The Woman who Lived her Life Backwards

ANN LEAHY

The Woman who Lived her Life Backwards

ARLEN
HOUSE

Published in 2008 by
ARLEN HOUSE
an imprint of Arlen Publications Ltd
PO Box 222
Galway
Phone/Fax: 353 86 8207617
Email: arlenhouse@gmail.com

Distributed in North America by
SYRACUSE UNIVERSITY PRESS
621 Skytop Road, Suite 110
Syracuse, NY 13244-5290
Phone: 315-443-5534/Fax: 315-443-5545
Email: supress@syr.edu

ISBN 978-1-903631-81-2, paperback
ISBN 978-1-903631-91-1, hardback
(a signed, numbered edition is also available)

Typesetting | Arlen House
Printing | Betaprint
Cover Image | Kathleen Furey

CONTENTS

for Rose Leahy

and in memory of
Tom Leahy and John Leahy

Acknowledgements

The core of this collection won the Patrick Kavanagh Award in 2001. Grateful acknowledgement is made to the editors of the following journals where some of these poems first appeared: *Agenda, Cyphers, Cathal Bui Anthology, Litspeak Dresden Vol IV, Orbis, Poetry Ireland Review, Poetry Society poetrynews, Stand, New Forest Poetry Society 2001, The SHOp, The Sunday Tribune, The New Welsh Review, The Collection 2000 (TNW)*.

Some poems were anthologised in the following books: Seamus Cashman (ed.), *Something Beginning with P: New Poems from Irish Poets* (Dublin, O'Brien Press, 2004, 2008). Antoinette Quinn (ed.), *Dancing with Kitty Stobling: An Anthology of the Patrick Kavanagh Award Winners, 1971–2003* (Dublin, Lilliput Press, 2004). *My Mother Threw Knives: An Anthology of Poems about Women's Lives* (London, Second Light, 2006). John Ennis (*et al*), *The Echoing Years: An Anthology of Poetry from Canada and Ireland* (Waterford, Centre for Newfoundland and Labrador Studies, 2007).

Some of these poems have been read on Lyric FM and on RTÉ Radio 1, and translated into Russian and Dutch.

For help and encouragement I acknowledge Seamus Cashman, Marianna Cullen, Phil Dineen, Anatoly Kudryavitsky, Miriam Lambe, Mamo McDonald, Janice Moore Fuller and Catherine Rose; Gerard Quinn and members of the Montrose poetry reading group; the late Pat Egan; and the Tyrone Guthrie Centre, Annamakerrig, Co. Monaghan. All my thanks to each member of my family.

The publisher acknowledges the support of Women's Education Bureau (WEB) in the publication of this book.

The Woman who Lived her Life Backwards

THE KALEIDOSCOPE MY BIG BROTHER GAVE ME

It created geometric processions out of rooms:
made a pair of butterflies rise from a fireside chair,
caused a ball of wool to fan and become a guelder rose,
a cylinder of gas to spoke into a four-pronged star,
eight eyes to glisten from a hot-plate ringed with chrome.

It put my reflection in as part of the pattern: let me see
myself in a pendulum, triangulated by a dour
mahogany surround. He helped me through a gap that year.
Finger to his lips, he slowed the whole summer down,
tuned out tractor drone, dog splash, sheep bleat –

moved in on one grasshopper sound, till we'd dipped
level with the angled systems of the insect's exterior,
its armoured legs jigging out an oscillating click
that swelled in the field, a chant rising in its cathedral.
I became a juggler of surfaces, an evangelist

of detail, my world broken down, re-configured. I'd take
rubbings from the paint tears hardened down our door, wait
outside, round the narrowing waterline, as polygons
broke out across the mud, baked by the sun.

MINCE CUSTOMER

Pinned to the door
was a diagram of a heifer
with sections straight-lined

across her side: sirloin
jigsawed between rib
and rump, shank slotting

into round. And the people
who came in, we sorted them
by the cuts they bought:

Mince customers wanted cosseting,
all the work done for them;
A fillet woman wanted only lean,

leaving all the fat
and gristle on our hands;
But a brisket man

was a prince, who'd take
his lean where he could get it
between the bone and thews.

Inside too a series of lines
ran through the house like skewers.
As a child you couldn't see them,

but bit by bit you'd puzzle out
the no-nonsense pattern they laid down,
plot yourself a course in which

your silverside was out
with your flank protected
your tenderloin concealed

or else you'd feel the chill
from the refrigeration unit
as sure as any mince customer.

SORCERER
for my mother

Jam jars baking in the oven
Bolsters boiling for apple jelly
Bread poultice to draw a splinter
Butter paper to line a loaf tin
Fish cakes for a Friday
Haliborange to curb the winter

She'd goad a ground-down tin-opener into cutting
Scoop a daddy-long-legs up in her fingers
Prise a tight-lipped lid from a jar of jam
Soft soap the twin-tub into jiggling and chuckling
Pluck the harm from a phrase over dinner
Tease roots from the stem of a geranium

We thought alchemy was something you took
with tea, that magic was made from cook-books.

FAIR GAME

Gun cases balanced
between chairs
in the kitchen.

Men assembling,
rods down the barrels
of their shotguns.

The metallic tang
of gun oil
above breakfast dishes.

Sandwiches being made
with corned beef.
Hard boiled eggs.

A child secreting
scraps of wadding
from a gun case

to twist around
her fingers
like a bandage,

watchful, aware
that a small thing
could set them off.

IN THE PRESSURE COOKER

For milestones there were appliances
umbilically attached to the wall.
Like the polisher that, early on,
would circle like a dancer out of control,

spreading wax in scarified rings,
around downstairs rooms,
the house charged and tense
from its fulminating roars,

or the twin-tub that meant a day
of sudsy puddles out the back
eventually breaking down
to make way for an automatic:

nine programmes, pre-rinse and spin.
One tight cube that took everything in
and drew no attention to itself
like well-behaved children.

When the pressure cooker
came, its manual
was read and read again,
its first spin and hiss a thrill,

everyone gathered round as if
to watch some young hopeful
perform. And the same fear –
that it might not settle

to a controlled release
of steam. Explode instead,
spray us all with shrapnel
from its stainless steel lid.

The kitchen became
a fluorescent-bulb shrine,
where Krups motors droned
beneath a steamy benediction,

those metallic pressure-cooked
stews – our staple. As long,
that is, as we could keep
the lid screwed down.

OFFSPRING OF AN ARTISAN GOD
i.m. of my father and of his father

'The end', he'd say, 'had more banter
in it than hammer, with hardly the scrape
of a rasp', leaving his children to ponder
a trade heroic in a mass-produced age;

how his glance might flash in a face smoked
tarmac-black; how a bar could curl and scroll,
if beaten in ringing, double-strokes,
if teased out, danced out on a dirt floor;

a neighbour's lad with all his weight
to crank the bellows as the air sways;
how on the up and the down beats
sparks would flay, sparks caught in eyes

inured to hot moods in iron work,
to slippery hot, or snowball hot,
to black hot glowing amber in the dark;
to spew and sizzle round the bosh;

to back-buckling, rough-wrought hours
of heave and tug; all the sweat and puff
of a working horse; on the nails, in the hair,
lining each pocket – the fug of scorched hoof.

And for a child, digging, to uncover?
Only horseshoes rusting in a tangle of weeds;
one thrumming pulse echoed by another;
gods at their ease in the family tree.

FORGED

A hammer, an anvil, a soldering iron:
these he left along with his name
given to the grandson born
the year he died and to the great grandson
who will never know either of them.
A name linking them in a chain

of forebears who exist as threads through
scraps of stories. But who knows
what we owe them? A crooked smile? A tilt
of the chin? A stubborn brow that keeps you
struggling on when everyone would let you go?
The past – it inhabits us. We live up to it,

react against it, fill out its prescription.
You skit around on gravel until you know
where you've been tethered all along:
outside the door of that forge.

THE TWISTED THREAD

'The twisted thread is stronger than the wind-swept fleece'
– Patrick Kavanagh, 'The Great Hunger'

What used to be taught were many arts.
How to measure a cut from a pound
of butter and never need a scales.
How to balance a blackberry tart
with sweet blacks and unripe reds.
How a tear in the pastry crust
would allow the juice to rise and scorch.
How to crop the lid and crimp its edge.

How to scald a pan, take the cold
out of milk for a litter. How to kill
a fly to feed a limp-winged bat;
how to do it when you know
they still die. How to salve nettle burns
using sap from a young stem. How to pluck
a tick from between a terrier's toes.
How to care, never betray it in words.

What to do with fruits too acerbic to eat:
damsons, elderberries, crabs.
How to drizzle hot syrup on a cold plate;
how to wait, watch the drops congeal,
pour a liquid, set it firm and jellied.
How gooseberries that stew to a mealy green
can be simmered to a lucid red preserve.
How to strip a bough of all its berries.

How to tell what's wrong with a clock
by listening to its whirrings and catchings.
How to file the weights of a long-case
and curb a pendulum's harried stroke.
How, in a house full of clocks, none were wound
though all were primed, capable of telling time.
How well-tuned parts, interlocking wheels,
need smooth bearings, feelings ringed round.

For what were feelings only pots
of milk boiled fit to overflow?
September wasps in the kitchen steam?
A blundering pup, its lead in knots?
Allow a cultivated bed to choke
with bindweed and what would you show
but hard work undone? How did we know
that love was no dandelion clock to blow?

Looking for Smoke Signs

I've come along this road
before, heading west from the ferry
following signs – Wexford,
New Ross, Thomastown, Kilkenny.

I take the route that seems most
straight, keep finding myself faced
with junctions at which signposts
are suddenly scarce.

Maybe it's meant to measure
how much I want to go this way?
On my own at night in the car
I tune in, hear my father say:

'Good to have tail-lights ahead
to make the road ... Take care
don't hug the ditch – you could
come on anything there'.

Advice put down ahead of time,
as I steered from the passenger seat.
He didn't live to see me get my turn
to work the pedals with my feet.

In Kilkenny – half-way there –
you have to find the road before
you see the sign. It seems to require
a kind of act of faith: I know

that once I find the turn
for Thurles, I'm home.

ORIENTATION LESSONS

We learn when young to trace a map,
to reproduce the crooked county line,
to recognise a way-marked track:
to grant a right of way across our lives.

A line or two suggests a cliff face
that's meant to be appeased and tiptoed round
or shades the body of a lake
we're never meant to go beyond.

We hear of townlands whose names
are never written down; instead they test
how we detect a boundary lane
that isolates one homestead from the next.

Later on, co-ordinates
recur; a tone of voice resounds.
It's the old grid we replicate
on a brand new stretch of ground.

It seems we took the only route we could:
long and steep – one we found we understood.

TEN STEPS ROUND

Your stick supports a wavering gait,
each aching step provokes a frown.
There's somewhere you must go, but wait

the garden's edge is smudged with rain
and pansies' heads caress the ground.
Your stick taps out the hours grown late:

that grasp holds firm, those cheeks still blaze.
Sleep now, I'll watch those ups and downs.
I sift for something I should raise

but rows of pills segment the days
and damp and drizzle muffle sounds.
That stick supports your sinking weight

from bed to window-pane to chair –
the world all done in ten steps round.
Nothing is news. So still the air

your craggy hill is partly veiled:
we cannot see its jagged end.
Your stick supports a wavering gait.
There's somewhere you must go, but wait.

He names the parts, offers no prognosis:
'could be a leak in the cooling system;
maybe damage to the cylinder head'.
The AA man considers his implements,
chooses his words. I watch him
lash the wheels to the tow truck,
remember the dealer's forecourt,
a line of cars, their paintwork gleaming,
you circling this one, taking stock.
You, by then, used to reading the silence
between words that were carefully chosen –
the mechanics of life or death responses.
The lurch as the truck is put in gear
and the car follows, inert,
is one more increment:
like recognising your writing
on a melted-down cassette,
or coming across your driving licence
in a drawer – past its expiry date.

COLD STORAGE

There was a cold room
at the back of our house.

Our father propped open the door
as sides of beef were shouldered
and sheep slit down their spines.

Speared on hooks they hung,
flanked by ox-tongues, long and thick
as a healthy man's thigh.

On the floor lay fleshy chickens
packed in boxes, their hearts and tumid
entrails bagged within their breasts.

Upstairs, you and I peered at the silver
fleck on a fish's eye in the kitchen
foreground of a painting by Velasquez,

or turned the page to trace the head
of John the Baptist through strips of greaseproof
meant to parcel out rack chops and T-bone steaks.

Later, after you and I had gone, our mother
scrubbed splatters of blood from the concrete,
hoovered the last flake of sawdust.

The room – windowless and airless
but no longer cold – stood empty but for
wool coats and leather jackets

that assembled there and hung
side-by-side like distant cousins
of the earlier occupants.

Now it's my turn to stand with my back
against the door, as the removal
men deliver boxes crammed

with kitchen knives, a fold-up barbecue,
your college thesis, Labour Party card,
out-sized atlas, home-made chess pieces.

Still wrapped in tissue, they lie on the floor,
in the dark, waiting ... to be sectioned up
portioned out, bartered with siblings

each one trying to piece the present
back together bit by bit; each one after
the thing that seems to have your heart in it.

LIME KILN COUNTRY

I come from limestone country
a bedrock that harbours
underground streams
and twisted ammonites
hard at its heart – old hurts
we spend our lives forgetting.

I come from limestone country
where there's a lime kiln
along every road and lane,
where rocks were rendered down
to whitewash houses, slake fields,
disinfect streets of all doubt.

I come from limestone country
where statues, cemented now
inside lime kilns, guard against
recollections that might sear
or stones that could be made
to give up their secrets.

LIVING WITH ST. PATRICK

There's a life-size figure of St. Patrick
– hand upraised, eyes downcast –
built-in to our modernised offices: relic
of the building's institutional past.

His cloak is snooker-table green
his expression ceramically detached
and if his crozier lacks its ancient sheen
his nails are still pink in their grasp.

Already on the phone we sometimes profess
more than we believe. We're afraid
in case some day we'll lapse and bless
ourselves if we turn up ten minutes late

that we'll give ourselves three Hail Marys
for being profligate with Post-its
that nothing will atone for a day
on which we make a cardinal mistake.

We're mounting a petition to look
for his taking down. Meanwhile we'll position
a screen to try and cover him up:
He's at odds with our corporate vision

and, besides, we've each already got
the mark of his staff through the foot.

THE WORRY CHEST

For years, I've kept a chest
of formal wear. I take it down
sometimes to see
what I might get rid of,
select a pair of slim high heels
with ankle strap constrictors,
choose a chiffon stole
almost too flimsy to fold
(and that never, in any case,
covered up much).

Then a feather – loose from a boa –
will spring at me, sink
to the floor in a little flutter
of unease. A strapless bra will hook
the netting of an underskirt
to plead its case. Raw silk
will fret at its seams,
and a zip in vintage georgette
will try to stop me in my tracks.
A boned bodice will imply

that we're all keeping something back –
its hems have bound it to secrecy.
I'll slam the lid, find
I'm fingering the beading
on a velvet purse as though
to pray over a series of old worries.
A pile of gauzy handkerchiefs
will end up on my landing
smelling of *Je Reviens,*
L'air du Temps, Obsession, Poison.

BOARDING PASS

They've given me another person's
boarding pass again.
Do they detect I'm keen
to see the world in someone else's skin?

To know how things seem
if you're the Mr Mulqueen
who, by now, must be
passing himself off as me?

They'll catch up with us both
in the end if we splash out
in the Duty Free, or forget
ourselves at the Departure Gate.

So if it cannot be
then change me back to me.
Only this time, if you can,
make me more like myself than I am.

RETROSPECT

A woman who was walking alone in the street,
saw a group of youngsters, heard the sound of running feet.
Pursued by a wolf whistle, she allowed herself a smile
and, turning, saw the look as his face dropped a mile.

Oh, what an unwanted pang you confront
when you find that you look younger
from the back than from the front.

ON FINDING NOTHING TO WEAR AT THE JANUARY SALES

It was as if
            her carefully
                      patterned life
had always been
               unravelling
                         to this point
and she fell
            backwards
                   down the escalator
from 'Young Miss'
               to bargain stall
                        lower ground floor.

If the Shoes Pinch …

The stilettos show
a hint of cleavage round the toe.

As the arches rise
each lacquered nail is poised

and pointed at the polished brogues next door
who no-one remembers meeting there before.

The brogues incline away
towards walking shoes in beige

– their host – to whom few pay heed
leaving him to wonder at the scuffing on the heels

of the little black courts with the uptight bows
and the squared-off toes.

The courts – sensible shoes – try to remain unmoved
by loafers slipped on along with well-worn views

and positioned to her right.
He, her date, keeps his shoes out of sight

and in the air is tapping out a separate theme
aimed at a pair of platform soles that seem

a bit ambitious to have been designed
to walk in – but made perhaps for a social incline.

Meanwhile high-laced ankle boots
in silence disapprove

especially of her husband – grey socks
in Birkenstocks –

who's still too busy tucking in
to let gimlet eyelets get to him.

Deciding to take her platforms seriously
the hostess interrupts with Earl Grey tea

anticipating trouble down below
where one stiletto hangs from just one toe

leaving a naked foot exposed
prepared to impose

on a brogue that'd rather be in step
with the host than with any of the guests.

Lacing his decaff, loosening his tongue
the host – oblivious – is ruminating on

the wax and buff of all his plans:
stilted conversation and life lived out in Timberlands.

CELLULITE BANDITS
for – but not about – my sisters

We are the cellulite bandits.
We threaten with a flash of thigh.
From editors of tabloids, we enquire
'Why stick to breasts if you like wobbly bits?'

We strut on beaches wearing scarlet
thongs, urging other bathers not to hide –
'Admit it, dimples do look cute on thighs'.
We are the cellulite bandits.

Coffee, clotted cream, chocolate with red wine –
we publish diets that are good for it,
campaign for stipple, champion wood chip
and threaten with a flash of thigh.

We raid department stores, mount pickets
over sales of firming gel. 'Choose Cellulite'
our placards say, 'Thigh-Dimple Pride'.
We are the cellulite bandits.

On Ruben's birthday, we arrange for picnics
at pool sides – dress optional. Guests vie
to win the titles 'Lumpiest', 'Ms Jellified'.
We are the cellulite bandits.
We threaten with a flash of thigh.

IF I WERE A CAT

I'd be the one
that draws back,
spits, splays her claws
at stretching hands
and bending faces,
that same cat
pursuing moths
on her own
in the dark
so that someone
might be drawn
to her display
of artful hops.

PULLING POWER

Outside, drizzle seems to generate
slugs to graze my dahlias' leaves.

Midnight, and silverfish escape
from the grout beneath my slippered feet.

Latent till some obscure deadline expires,
weevils appear in my last ounce of rice.

Viruses, bacteria in the veins
wait for the defences to grow weak

as self-doubts, vague misgivings, wait
till the world deals a blow. Unforeseen,

this setback, though familiar when it strikes:
you've been a magnet for it all your life.

A House Divided

I'm applying paper to the window panes
pouring boiling water down the outflow pipes
sealing off the air vents with Vaseline
muzzling the letter box with masking tape;
I've given up feeling bad about men.

I've plastered putty round the back door frame
ditched the doormat in the hawthorn hedge
filled a skip with high heels, flimsy underwear
buried cut stems in the sweet pea bed;
I can't see any further use for them.

I won't unhook the security chain
when my groceries come from Tesco.
I'll slip the boy a tip and wait for him
to go before I open back the door;
No one will ever get to me again.

Once my email's disconnected, I'll turn on
the PC – not living I'll want to write about it
not feeling I'll find myself imagining
it, my effusions saved to floppy disc;
I'll never be in need of anything.

Feelings I will then confine to drawers, not loose
in the house careering up the gable
walls like cracks. But sorted as to source,
labelled 'good', 'bad' or 'grey & intangible'.
I'm hoping for lots of the latter; of course,
I've given up feeling.

TWO WALKS
'... a lifetime of
Taking real things for shadows'
– Bernard O'Donoghue, 'Ter Conatus'

I

Pink, the rambling cabbage rose.
Pressed against her face,
its kitchen-garden scent
masks the country-road redolence

of hogweed, elder, feverfew.
Sown, perhaps, to greet
comers round a gate,
or to overhang a cottage door,

no masonry remains of the home
recalled in this unfurling
between blackthorn and sycamore –
a rose contending year on year.

II

Bruise-black, the sloes that she
once picked, their bloom opaque.
Her young man knew no more and bit.
Acrid, the effluvium that seared ...

Though he made to pin her arms,
kiss the tartness back, she'd caught
his first puzzled look,
remembers it. In love then

with her own anonymous routes
through an untried city,
she was liable to take
solid walls for their shadows.

III

Now, unruly strands nudge
the parallel lines of her decisions:
she's surprised by the clear blue
of periwinkle, the hot orange of montbretia.

CAUSTIC SODA

There's pure peroxide in her veins
they swear who've seen her bleed;
they're sure that she could free-up drains
from her bathtub if she sneezed.

It's said that when she deigns to sweat
it smells of cider vinegar
and that if you could distil her breath
you'd discover oil of vitriol.

What isn't known is that if she cried
you'd see drops of glycerine,
for her heart is in formaldehyde
and her tears are never seen.

In The Shallows

In the shallows tadpoles wriggle
        to the surface – gasp for air.
Beside them stand a couple
        – they're a recently formed pair.

She lets him take her arm
        though his eyes are turned away:
He's scanning her reflection
        for anything it might betray.

They too are being observed:
        a Heron Crane waits above.
Below she waits for just one word
        and only hears its absence – love.

The bird resumes its stand
        as they go on ahead.
Though nothing's said they understand
        that something's newly dead.

SPIDERMAN

Here he is at the centre of his web,
each claw pressed against a radial rib.
A flutter from a passing fruit fly's wing
oscillates along the length of all his limbs,
causes a throb inside his poison duct;
his joints tense against the shock of impact.

Here he is at the centre of his web.
Alone, he's in on the secrets of its threads –
those that glisten and stick, how well
they've each been twisted, flexed in parallel,
how he's kept so busy with repairs,
how he's been keeping it all in place for years.

Yet he does it all at an automatic glide
as though across the surface of his life
every tendon working double-quick
every step he takes – one you could predict.

BOLSTERED

These nights
I go to bed
with a grudge.

I keep putting
my hands to it
turning it over

wrapping it up
to keep
the heat in it.

Each night
I top it up
in the kitchen

rerun
scenes
in my head

screw
my resentment
in tight

towel off
stray signs
of weakness.

It keeps me company
– my grudge –
keeps me here

on my own
braced against
the air.

Traditional Irish Folk Wisdom *(with variation)*

Know a man for seven years before you stoke his fire.
Stoke a man for seven years before you know his fire.
Fire a man for seven years before you know his stoke.
Man his stoke for seven years before you fire his know.

For seven years, stoke a man before his fire.
Before you fire a man, know his stoke for seven years.
Seven years before you know, a man will fire his stoke.

EMPTY SETTING

A pearl fell
from one of your earrings today.

The empty setting
grazed my fingers

as I waited, restless,
for the lights to change.

The pair you gave me at Christmas
intended as a bribe.

I slipped them off in the rear-view mirror
and put them down.

They're still there now
lolling, noncommittal, on the dash.

Better to be bare than lopsided.

My Life as a Wardrobe

Clothes-hangers line up, each one
a collarbone inside a form of who
I used to be or who I'd like to be.

Mistakes of seasons past
trail from those I try
not to take down anymore:

a cashmere twin set
I didn't care for;
a halter-top that came

with strings attached;
a hound's-tooth suit
that never flattered me.

Meanwhile aspirations glitter
from evening dresses I confine
to plastic transparencies.

Who I am depends on several
mismatched hangers at one end.
There never seem to be enough.

This year's losses and gains are on display
as separates that coordinate, their stitching
under strain at the top of a side slit.

Time going by I recognise in shapes
too wide on the shoulders
too short on the thigh

or in a jacket whose stress line on the hips
is becoming a permanent wrinkle
like the one between my brows

or like that semi-invisible seam
between what is and what might have been.

FOR THE DINNER GUEST
starting and ending with a line by Keats

This living hand, now warm and capable
of a thousand tender touches tends
to spend them on mortise locks and ice-cube trays.
It's intimate with indicator sticks and steering wheels.
For you it's spent all day buffing glasses
for the wine, caressing stainless steel.
Here's a fork I fondled earlier;
I hold it towards you.

WINTER SOLSTICE?

Stone still in bed the morning of that day
concentric semi-circles in a clammy embrace

– our last; the digital clock
having long since gone off.

A shaft of sunlight escaped around
a chink at the edge of the blackout blind,

pierced the gloom and caught me unprepared,
remade my room as the central chamber

in Newgrange. And though supporting a wintry
leadenness, aware that in me

there'd been signs of a thaw, and sensing
on my mouth the trace of a yes.

TIGHT FIT

Why did her red dress suddenly aspire to a life of its own?
It was letting its shoulder straps down, easing open
its series of buttons, putting too much strain on its stitching.

And her sensible shoes, why did they seem keen
to head out in unlikely directions? To go up
down-escalators? To get a bit lost on a circular walk?

She was puzzled that her duvet cover
would slip off the bed – all easy in its amplitude,
all cosy with its crevices – to hug an old boot on the floor.

The tacks holding her picture backs in place were silently
                                        edging free.
She worried that her window blind might soon capitulate,
spring and put her on display, barefoot, in her underwear.

A Good Rogeting

I keep to myself on one side of a bed.
Its other half is occupied by books
meant to match my moods, catch the thread
of all my thoughts, from hard-angled works
of reference, to magazines, loose leaf pads.
A collection of love-lorn verse
hugs an impenetrable masterpiece
while Judith Hearne's eclipsed by glamour ads.

When I bring a new one back
over dinner with a glass of wine
I imagine removing its paper bag
running my fingers down its spine
how I'll fan the pages to inhale
its pristine smell, then make it my own:
easing back the sleeve and going down
on the biographical detail.

Sometimes that's the best bit
on evenings when I'm not in form
to get stuck in or to commit
not even to paper. One volume
alone then seems able to interject:
Chambers Twentieth Century Dictionary –
something new with every read
and no long-term effects.

I can fall asleep over a phrase whose
meaning remains a stranger and wake
in the morning with *Roget's Thesaurus*
poking me urgently in the back.

BEYOND THE PALE
in West Cork

I commit a minor act of appropriation –
pick plants whose names I don't know
from the ditches to try and make my own
of the unfamiliar:
the rise ahead in the road
the peak of Miskish behind me
the arthritic finger of Coulagh bay before me.

In my field guide I always seem
to be going over the same ground:
heath speedwell, scabious, lady's bedstraw.
Words from a language I speak
that remain as foreign as the names
for parts of speech: possessive pronouns,
complex prepositions – the past imperfect.

I consult *Ó Dónaill*, roll the Irish names
around my mouth like bullseyes:
anuallach, cab an ghasáin, boladh cnis,
words that sound familiar
from a language I don't speak,
whose sense is raw around the edge –
plucked stems themselves.

Note:
anuallach – speedwell – lit. arrogance
cab an ghasáin – scabious – lit. toothless mouth of the sprig
boladh cnis – *lady's bedstraw – lit. smell of skin*

RULES OF ATTRACTION

Two hard consonants rarely observed
out together cheek by jowl.
They rub each other up the wrong way:
inside the confines of a single word
they seem to need, between them, the play
allowed by a series of vowels.

Yet here they are again in print –
initial letters, two names, bunk-bedded
at the back of a poetry review,
alphabetical order seeming to flaunt
an easy intimacy between the two,
making their owners stop, muddle-headed

as to why – when the two of them have learnt
to keep apart, dealings cordial but distant –
do their separate submissions made at random
hit their targets together, come off in tandem?

BELEAGUERED

There's a mite attacking all the bees
in Ireland: the *do bes* and the *don't bes*
the *does bes* and the *doesn't bes*.
It's come in from abroad
but now it's in the blood
passed from one to the next
leaving a whole colony stunted,
hyper-correct. On its last legs –
this strain of the habitual present tense.

POLICING THE WASTE GROUND
*'The great majority of introduced plants occur on waste
or disturbed ground ...'*
– Fitter *et al, Wild Flowers of Britain and Northern Europe*

At sixty miles an hour she found
that she looked down on plants
of waste ground – bastard agrimony,
common mallow, prickly poppies –
and on the magpies that patrol
the margins of the N4 road.

At thirty miles an hour abreast
a bridge she'd crossed a thousand times
before, she faced a ruined keep
wedged – like an incongruous belief –
between a family grocers
and a general hardware store.

At ten miles an hour, skirting a bend
above the town that she grew up in,
she observed that she was still
attached to bramble, hawthorn,
robin-run-the-hedge; to dog rose,
fetid woundwort, carrion crows.

At a full stop inside her old room,
she knew that there were fledgling
views that she confined to her own
wayside places, to derelict
urban sites of her own mind:
how her native species of thought

had its own magpies
always on the look out.

MORNING GLORY
Bindweed

The shape of invitation;
such a yawning, out-bending in bloom,
each white neck rising from a pair of bracts
that taper like an *haute couture* neckline.
These, your flowers, are bride-like:

they have their one big day
when they must embody radiance.
If they could talk, they'd cry,
'Love me. Enter. Now'.
The hawk-moth or the bee

that does will know constraint
in the sharply narrowing neck,
the *cheval-de-frise* of the pistil,
consummation denied to all
but the longest-tongued.

Having no backbone, you would go
on your belly, but you are juiced,
in a frenzy for ascent. Your leaves
are spearmen – all angles
cover your advance.

Displaced aristocrat, you are
the roadside undertow,
despising the coarse blade,
the common shoot on whom
your rise depends, careless

whether your corkscrewing
strangles or stunts. Banished
to the garden's furthest reaches
you can, if pulled, uproot
your host for spite.

Your sour milk-sap,
arched edge of each corolla,
twist of each tendril, is honed
for seduction and conquest,
hardened to murder and rape.

THE SEASON
for G. who says that wild flowers aren't sexy

Long-lashed celandine lowers her petals,
shy of spring chills; her leaves describe
a heart that's been blunted. Silverweed
– downy underneath, sharp-toothed at the edges –
scopes the undergrowth for ground
she hasn't yet turned over. Competition's steep.
Bugloss can bristle and graze and, where
midribs are bare, nodes can be swollen.

Vetch lassos young blades, clambers to get
within reach with blue finger-flowers, leaves
that are lances. Vanilla-scented meadowsweet's
a tease, exposing her anthers, suggesting
a summer ceremony in lace. Solitary loosestrife
is complicated – a lot goes on in rhizomes
underground. Despite links with honey, clover's
never sweet; those leaves love their threesomes.

Purple panicles drape the stems of nettles
– cravats on the necks of old roués. They still
like to sting. Some lose their shirts,
but shepherd's purse is constant year-round,
his heart on his sleeve. Stragglers in the heel
of the year, cleavers hang round to cadge a ride.
Hart's tongues lick the air. Many opt to self-pollinate.
Perennials shrink to crowns. Seeds go to ground.

WHAT A POET NOTICES

'One of the attractions of lichens is the range of colours
they exhibit which may be why poets ... notice them'
– Oliver Gilbert, *Lichens*

I notice their hob-goblin greens,
their scarlet pixie cups,
plaques of reindeer rust.
But it's not that so much as how they seem
to hug a rock so close you'd think
they're in its grain. It's how you can detect
them where you least expect:
a sewer works wall with spots of tar or ink,
a bloom on a log in the undergrowth.
It's how they resist definition –
not moss, liverwort, nor fern,
not alga or fungus, but bit of both.
It's not the range of colours they display.
It's their touch of other-world in the everyday.

WISHING LINES

I put words down along a line
hoping for a turn of phrase
that will whisk them off and away
to snatch a sigh from a telegraph wire,

catch the burble of a broken main,
a patch of sunlight from a two-tiered
interchange, swirl them back to me,
trailing a whiff of mugwort, a trace

of old-man's-beard, and carrying an overtone
of something I haven't yet pegged down.

The Woman who Lived her Life Backwards
'for as a child I knew I was no child
as now I know I am not old'
– Doug Fetherling, 'Elijah Speaking'

As a shadow unpeels itself
across a mountain, or a red balloon
drifts loose from its owner's grasp,
I am in love again. In love
with the startled look
sheep have after shearing,
with a cobweb unravelling
on the breeze, crab apple
in bud behind railings,
that mossy river-smell after a flood.

If I could touch this paling
erected all around me,
I would build instead a raft,
fling it on the swell.
I would let the course find me.
My indifference dissolving, my reserve
unstrung, I would unloose
wonder wherever I was led.
Then my heart would unstitch itself.
I would every day grow young.